CONTEÚDO DIGITAL PARA ALUNOS

Cadastre-se e transforme seus estudos em uma experiência única de aprendizado:

1

Entre na página de cadastro:
https://sistemas.editoradobrasil.com.br/cadastro

2

Além dos seus dados pessoais e dos dados de sua escola, adicione ao cadastro o código do aluno, que garantirá a exclusividade do seu ingresso à plataforma.

1499992A1712196

3

Depois, acesse:
https://leb.editoradobrasil.com.br/
e navegue pelos conteúdos digitais de sua coleção **:D**

Lembre-se de que esse código, pessoal e intransferível, é valido por um ano. Guarde-o com cuidado, pois é a única maneira de você acessar os conteúdos da plataforma.

Editora do Brasil

BRINCANDO
COM INGLÊS

1

EDUCAÇÃO
INFANTIL

RENATO MENDES CURTO JÚNIOR

Licenciado em Letras

Certificado de proficiência em Língua Inglesa pela Universidade de Michigan e TOEFL

Autor de livros de educação a distância

Professor de Língua Inglesa e Portuguesa na rede particular de ensino desde 1986

ANNA CAROLINA GUIMARÃES

Licenciada em Pedagogia

Especialista em Educação Infantil e Anos Iniciais

Especialista em neuropsicopedagogia

Coordenadora pedagógica de Educação Básica

CIBELE MENDES

Mestre em Educação

Licenciada em Pedagogia

Certificado de proficiência em Língua Inglesa pela Fluency Academy

Coordenadora pedagógica de Educação Infantil aos Anos Finais do Ensino Fundamental

Editora do Brasil

Dados Internacionais de Catalogação na Publicação (CIP)
(Câmara Brasileira do Livro, SP, Brasil)

Curto Júnior, Renato Mendes
Brincando com inglês: educação infantil 1 / Renato Mendes Curto Júnior, Anna Carolina Guimarães, Cibele Mendes. – 5. ed. – São Paulo: Editora do Brasil, 2024. – (Brincando com)

ISBN 978-85-10-09507-5 (aluno)
ISBN 978-85-10-09508-2 (professor)

1. Educação infantil I. Guimarães, Anna Carolina. II. Mendes, Cibele. III. Título. IV. Série.

24-193057 CDD-372.21

Índices para catálogo sistemático:

1. Educação infantil 372.21
Eliane de Freitas Leite - Bibliotecária - CRB-8/8415

5ª edição / 1ª impressão, 2024
Impresso na Hawaii Gráfica e Editora

Editora do Brasil

Avenida das Nações Unidas, 12901
Torre Oeste, 20º andar
São Paulo, SP – CEP: 04578-910
Fone: +55 11 3226-0211
www.editoradobrasil.com.br

Direção-geral: Paulo Serino de Souza

Diretoria editorial: Felipe Ramos Poletti
Gerência editorial de conteúdo didático: Erika Caldin
Gerência editorial de produção e design: Ulisses Pires
Supervisão de design: Aurélio Gadini Camilo
Supervisão de arte: Abdonildo José de Lima Santos
Supervisão de revisão: Elaine Cristina da Silva
Supervisão de iconografia: Léo Burgos
Supervisão de digital: Priscila Hernandez
Supervisão de controle e planejamento editorial: Roseli Said
Supervisão de direitos autorais: Luciana Sposito

Supervisão editorial: Carla Felix Lopes e Diego da Mata
Edição: Danuza D. Gonçalves, Graziele Arantes, Natália Feulo e Sheila Fabre
Assistência editorial: Igor Gonçalves e Julia do Nascimento
Revisão: 2014 Soluções Editoriais, Alexander Barutti, Andréia Andrade, Beatriz Dorini, Gabriel Ornelas, Giovana Sanches, Jonathan Busato, Júlia Castelo, Maisa Akazawa, Mariana Paixão, Martin Gonçalves, Rita Costa, Rosani Andreani e Sandra Fernandes
Pesquisa iconográfica: Maria Santos e Selma Nagano
Tratamento de imagens: Robson Mereu
Projeto gráfico: Siamo Studio
Capa: Caronte Design
Imagem de capa: Graziela Andrade
Edição de arte: Daniele Fátima Oliveira e Yara Penteado Espírito Santo Anderi
Ilustrações: Bambrilla Ilustra, Bruno Okada, Claudia Marianno, Carolina Sartório, DKO Estúdio, Ideario Lab, Janete Trindade, Luiz Lentini, Maíra Nakazaki, Marcelo Azalim e Patricia Paulozi
Editoração eletrônica: Ab Aeterno
Licenciamentos de textos: Cinthya Utiyama, Ingrid Granzotto, Renata Garbellini e Solange Rodrigues
Controle e planejamento editorial: Ana Fernandes, Bianca Gomes, Juliana Gonçalves, Maria Trofino, Terezinha Oliveira e Valéria Alves

APRESENTAÇÃO

QUERIDO ALUNO,

ESTE É O **BRINCANDO COM INGLÊS** EM SUA MAIS NOVA VERSÃO, PARA QUE O APRENDIZADO DA LÍNGUA INGLESA SE TORNE AINDA MAIS DIVERTIDO!

VOCÊ ENCONTRARÁ ATIVIDADES ESTIMULANTES E VIVENCIARÁ SITUAÇÕES DO DIA A DIA, PARA ESCUTAR, FALAR E APRENDER INGLÊS DE MODO NATURAL.

CADA AULA SERÁ UMA NOVA EXPERIÊNCIA, E VOCÊ NÃO VAI QUERER PARAR DE APRENDER!

VAMOS COMEÇAR?

OS AUTORES

CONHEÇA SEU LIVRO

SEJA BEM-VINDO À NOVA EDIÇÃO DO **BRINCANDO COM INGLÊS**!

LET'S START

LOCALIZADA NO INÍCIO DE CADA VOLUME, ESTA SEÇÃO APRESENTA ATIVIDADES LÚDICAS QUE POSSIBILITAM PREPARAR OS ALUNOS PARA OS NOVOS CONTEÚDOS, RETOMANDO TÓPICOS JÁ VISTOS.

LET'S PLAY

A SEÇÃO PROPÕE ATIVIDADES LÚDICAS RELACIONADAS À TEMÁTICA DA UNIDADE, COMO JOGO DE ERROS, APLICAÇÃO DE ADESIVOS ETC.

STICKERS

ADESIVOS PARA OS ALUNOS COLAREM EM DETERMINADAS ATIVIDADES.

LET'S LISTEN

O ALUNO TERÁ A OPORTUNIDADE DE OUVIR ÁUDIOS COM DIÁLOGOS E CANÇÕES, PARA SE HABITUAR COM A LÍNGUA INGLESA.

GOOD DEED

APRESENTA TEMÁTICAS DE CUNHO SOCIAL E ÉTICO RELACIONADAS AO ASSUNTO DE CADA UNIDADE. CONTEMPLA OS OBJETIVOS DE APRENDIZAGEM E DESENVOLVIMENTO PREVISTOS NA BNCC PARA A EDUCAÇÃO INFANTIL.

DIGITAL PLAY

A SEÇÃO PROPÕE ATIVIDADES QUE INCLUEM O USO DE TECNOLOGIA, QUE SERÃO ORIENTADAS E ACOMPANHADAS PELO PROFESSOR.

LET'S SING

A SEÇÃO PROPÕE CANÇÕES PARA O ALUNO OUVIR E CANTAR.

AFTER THIS UNIT I CAN

A SEÇÃO OFERECE AO ALUNO A OPORTUNIDADE DE FAZER UMA AUTOAVALIAÇÃO, ENTENDENDO OS PONTOS EM QUE ENCONTROU MAIS FACILIDADE OU MAIS DIFICULDADE.

VOCABULARY

VOCABULÁRIO BILÍNGUE COM OS VOCÁBULOS ESTUDADOS NOS TEXTOS APRESENTADOS.

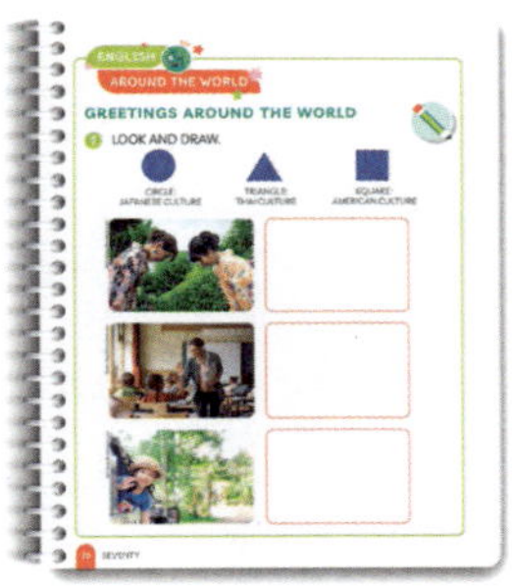

ENGLISH AROUND THE WORLD

A SEÇÃO CONTEMPLA A DIMENSÃO INTERCULTURAL DA LÍNGUA INGLESA, DESTACANDO OS ASPECTOS CULTURAIS DE PAÍSES QUE UTILIZAM O INGLÊS COMO IDIOMA OFICIAL OU LÍNGUA FRANCA.

REVIEW

AS ATIVIDADES DESTA SEÇÃO PROPÕEM A RETOMADA DO CONTEÚDO ESTUDADO.

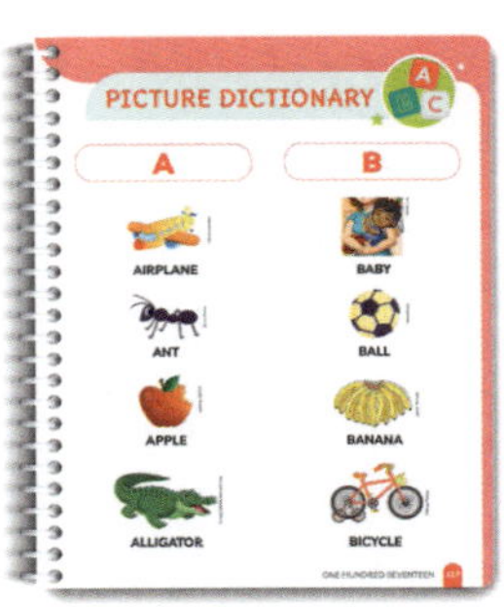

PICTURE DICTIONARY

A SEÇÃO DISPONIBILIZA O VOCABULÁRIO ESTUDADO NO LIVRO E AS RESPECTIVAS IMAGENS.

CELEBRATIONS

ENCARTE QUE INCLUI ATIVIDADES RELACIONADAS A DATAS COMEMORATIVAS.

ÍCONES

DESENHAR	COLORIR	FALAR OU CONVERSAR	TRAÇAR OU ESCREVER
CANTAR	ADESIVO	DESTAQUE	CIRCULAR
MARCAR	CONTAR	ESCUTAR	ENCONTRAR
COLAR	RECORTAR	LIGAR/ RELACIONAR	APONTAR

CONTENTS

LET'S START!

1 GET TO KNOW YOUR NEW FRIENDS. PASTE THE STICKERS.

Arquivo do autor

RODA-GIGANTE EM NIAGARA FALLS. CANADÁ, 2023.

2 HELP THE GIRLS GET TO THE DINOSAUR PARK.

Ideario Lab

Arquivo do autor

3 FIND FIVE DIFFERENCES.

Ideario Lab

4 FIND AND CIRCLE THE ODD ONE OUT.

A)

Alex Staroseltsev/Shutterstock.com

lefthanderman/Shutterstock.com

B)

Melinda Nagy/Shutterstock.com

oksana2010/Shutterstock.com

C)

Sports and Leather/Shutterstock.com

FocusStocker/Shutterstock.com

5 CIRCLE THE GIRLS WITH RED AND THE BOYS WITH GREEN.

Ideario Lab

ERIC

JAY

AVA

SOPHIA

TIM

MIA

6 WHAT ANIMAL IS THIS? LOOK AND TRACE.

Arquivo do autor

DINOSAUR

7 COLOR THE KIDS WITH A BALL.

8 COLOR YOUR FAVORITE FRUIT.

Ideario Lab

9 CIRCLE THE GREEN ANIMALS.

nu kristie/Shutterstock.com

Teguh Mujiono/Shutterstock.com

Svesla Tasla/Shutterstock.com

Muhammad Desta Laksana/Shutterstock.com

shahadatarman 0/Shutterstock.com

yusufdemirci/Shutterstock.com

UNIT 1

ALL ABOUT ME

VOCABULARY

WELCOME: BEM-VINDO(A).
CLASS: TURMA.
I AM: EU SOU.
SWIMMING TEACHER: PROFESSOR(A) DE NATAÇÃO.
HELLO: OLÁ.
MISS: SENHORITA.
HI: OI.
GOOD AFTERNOON: BOA TARDE.
SWIMMING: NATAÇÃO.

LET'S PLAY

1. CIRCLE THE KIDS WHO ARE PLAYING IN PAIRS.

Ideario Lab

2. TRACE THE WORDS.

- IN THE PARK THERE ARE FOUR GIRLS.

GIRLS

- IN THE PARK THERE ARE FOUR BOYS.

BOYS

DIGITAL PLAY

MY FAVORITE GANG!

Rawpixel.com/Shutterstock.com

1. GET TOGETHER WITH YOUR CLASSMATES FOR A CLASS PHOTO.

2. TRACE THE WORDS.

CLASS

FAVORITE

GANG

ENGLISH AROUND THE WORLD

DIFFERENT GREETINGS AROUND THE WORLD

1 CIRCLE THE WORDS.

Sergey Novikov/Shutterstock.com

2 TRACE THE WORD.

HELLO

LET'S PLAY

1 PASTE THE STICKERS. THEN COLOR THE WORDS.

I AM A...

BOY

I AM A...

GIRL

Ilustrações Claudia Marianno

2 TRACE THE SENTENCES.

I AM A BOY

I AM A GIRL

LET'S LISTEN

1 LISTEN AND REPEAT.

ERIC IS A BOY.

MEET THE BOYS AND A GIRL FROM ERIC'S CLASS!

HELLO.
I AM JAY.
I AM A BOY.

HI.
I AM SOPHIA.
I AM A GIRL.

HELLO.
I AM TIM.
I AM A BOY.

2 MATCH THE CHILDREN WITH THE SENTENCES.

Ideario Lab

HELLO,
I AM BECKY.

I AM A GIRL.

HI, I AM JAY.

HELLO,
I AM TIM.

I AM A BOY.

HI, I AM MIA.

3 PASTE THE STICKERS AND SAY IF IT'S A BOY OR A GIRL.

Ideario Lab

LET'S SING!

GIRLS AND BOYS COME OUT TO PLAY

GIRLS AND BOYS COME OUT TO PLAY,
THE MOON DOTH SHINE AS BRIGHT AS DAY,
LEAVE YOUR SUPPER, AND LEAVE YOUR SLEEP,
AND JOIN YOUR PLAYFELLOWS INTO THE STREET.

COME WITH A WHOOP, COME WITH A CALL,
COME WITH A GOOD WILL, OR NOT AT ALL.
UP THE LADDER AND DOWN THE WALL,
A PENNY LOAF WILL SERVE US ALL.

POPULAR SONG.

Ideario Lab

GOOD DEED

GIRLS AND BOYS COME OUT TO PLAY WITH RESPECT!

- LOOK AT THE PICTURE WITH HAPPY CHILDREN PLAYING TOGETHER.

Pressmaster/Shutterstock.com

AFTER THIS UNIT

I CAN

GREET PEOPLE.			
IDENTIFY *BOYS* AND *GIRLS*.			
USE *MY NAME IS...*			
IDENTIFY COLORS.			

UNIT 2

MY NAME

Ideario Lab

VOCABULARY

HELLO: OLÁ!

MY NAME IS: MEU NOME É.

WHAT: QUAL.

HI: OI!

I AM: EU SOU.

LET'S PLAY

1 COLOR THE PICTURE. YOU ARE...

A GIRL　　A BOY

Stepan Gusiev/Shutterstock.com

2 YOUR BEST FRIEND IS...

( ) A GIRL

Olga1818/Shutterstock.com

( ) A BOY

A GIRL　　A BOY

LET'S LISTEN

1 SAY THE LETTERS AND COLOR THEM.

A E I

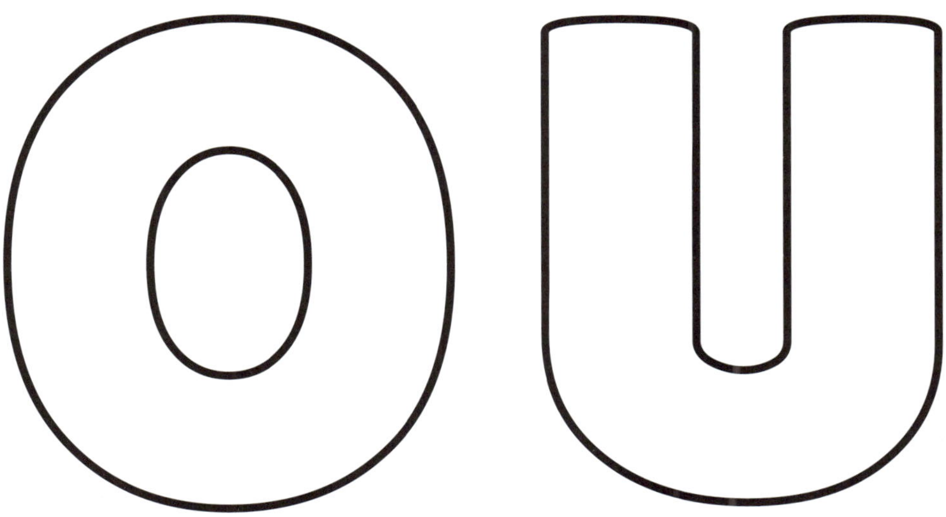

O U

LET'S PLAY

1 TRACE THE LETTERS.

GraphicsRF/Shutterstock.com

A

ANT

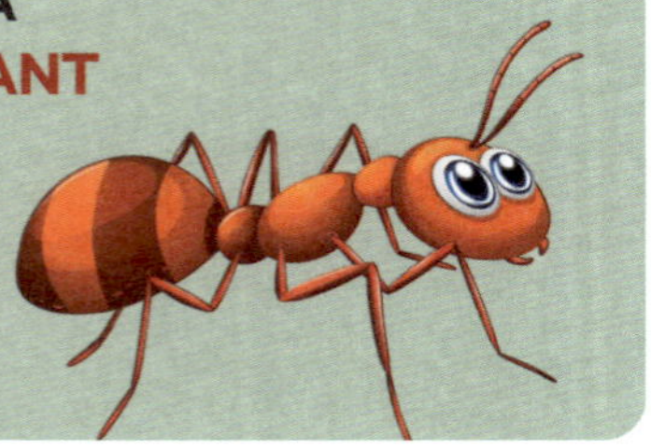

Nataly HK /Shutterstock.com

E

ELEPHANT

Granate Art /Shutterstock.com/

I

IGLOO

Andriy Lipkan/Shutterstock.com

O

ONION

goodwin_x/Shutterstock.com

U

UMBRELLA

2 FIND THE LETTERS AND COLOR THEM.

Claudia Marianno

3 WRITE THE MISSING LETTER.

PinkPeng/Shutterstock.com

G _ RL

Olleg Visual Content/Shutterstock.com

B _ Y

4 TRACE AND COLOR THE LETTER **A**.

comfuatprasetya/Shutterstock.com

AIRPLANE

Vector Cool Arts/Shutterstock.com

ALLIGATOR

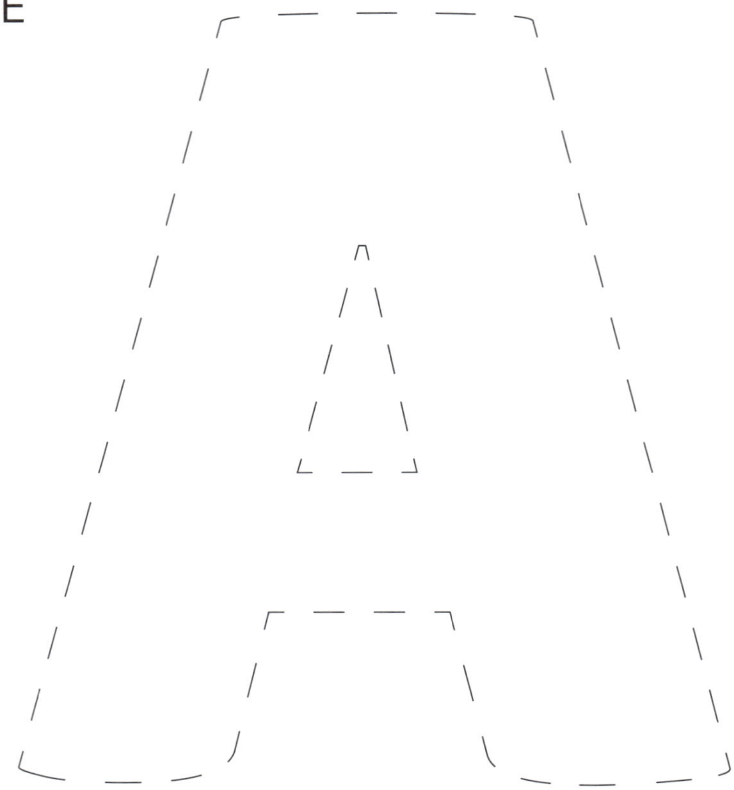

Victoria Sergeeva/Shutterstock.com

APPLE

GraphicsRF/Shutterstock.com

ANT

5 TRACE AND COLOR THE LETTER **E**.

BlueRingMedia/ Shutterstock.com

EGG

FARBAI/Shutterstock.com

ERASER

InkztingStduio ID/ Shutterstock.com

EAGLE

Mimosastudio/ Shutterstock.com

ELEPHANT

6 TRACE AND COLOR THE LETTER I.

ABC vector/
Shutterstock.com

ICE CREAM

BlueRingMedia/
Shutterstock.com

IGLOO

Vector Cool Arts/
Shutterstock.com

IGUANA

Vertes Edmond Mihai/
Shutterstock.com

INSECT

7 TRACE AND COLOR THE LETTER **O**.

PK Designs/
Shutterstock.com

ONION

ivelly/Shutterstock.com

ORANGE

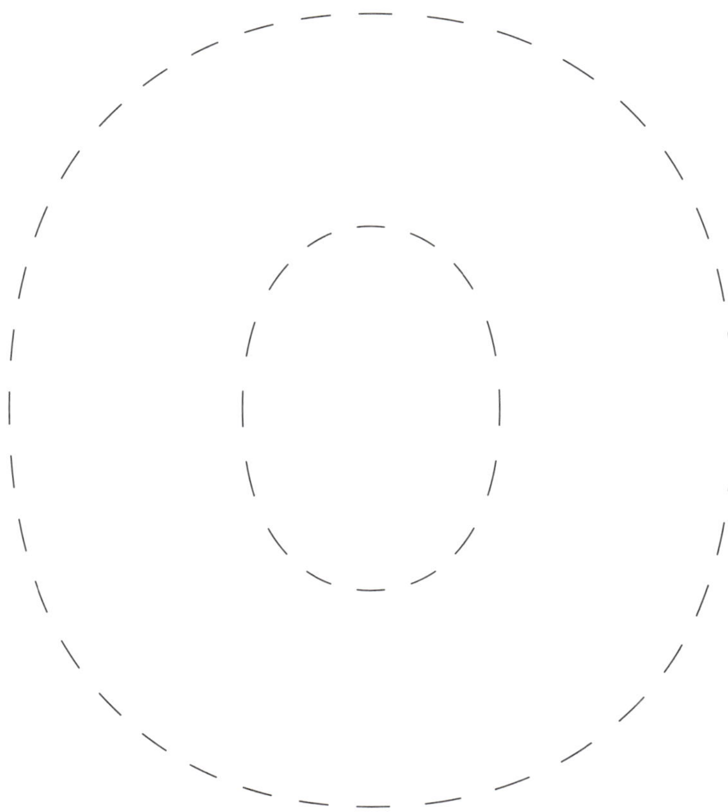

Zaleman/Shutterstock.com

OWL

ianlusung/Shutterstock.com

OCTOPUS

8 TRACE AND COLOR THE LETTER **U**.

hvostik/Shutterstock.com/

UMBRELLA

mako/iStockphoto.com

UNIFORM

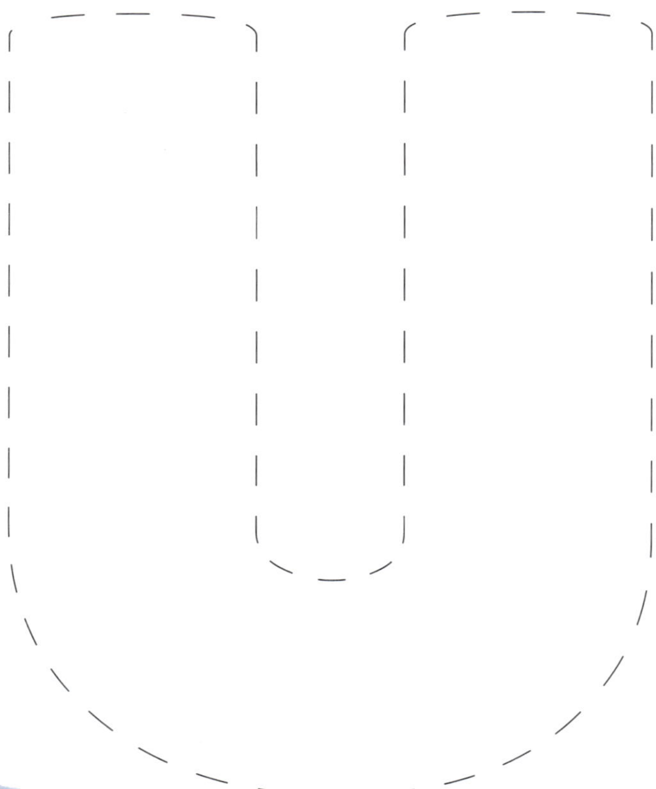

Claudia Marianno

UNIVERSITY

charnsitr/Shutterstock.com

USA FLAG

LET'S LISTEN

1. LISTEN AND COLOR THE PICTURES.

Astarina/Shutterstock.com

AIRPLANE

Tetiana Kopyl/Shutterstock.com

ELEPHANT

wnprh collective/Shutterstock.com

ICE CREAM

Irene_A/Shutterstock.com

ORANGE

VectorSun/Shutterstock.com/

UMBRELLA

LET'S PLAY

1 CONNECT THE DOTS AND TRACE THE CHILDREN'S NAMES.

Ideario Lab

MIA ERIC

LET'S SING!

ABC SONG

A - B - C - D - E - F - G
H - I - J - K - L - M - N - O - P
Q - R - S - T - U - V
W - X - Y AND Z
THESE ARE THE LETTERS FROM "A TO Z".
NOW THEY ARE PART OF ME.

TRADITIONAL NURSERY RHYME. ADAPTED.

Ideario Lab

VOCABULARY

LETTERS: LETRAS.
NOW: AGORA.
PART OF ME: PARTE DE MIM.

DIGITAL PLAY

NAMES AROUND THE WORLD

- WRITE A NAME FROM YOUR RESEARCH.

Roman Samborskyi/Shutterstock.com

AFTER THIS UNIT

I CAN

INTRODUCE MYSELF (*HELLO/HI*).			
USE *MY NAME IS... /I AM...*			
IDENTIFY THE VOWEL SOUNDS.			
IDENTIFY GIRLS AND BOYS.			

UNIT 3

LET'S COUNT!

Ideario Lab

VOCABULARY

JUMPING ROPE (TO JUMP): PULANDO CORDA (PULAR).

COUNT (TO COUNT): CONTE (CONTAR).

ONE: UM.

TWO: DOIS.

THREE: TRÊS.

FOUR: QUATRO.

FIVE: CINCO.

LET'S PLAY

1. PASTE THE STICKERS. THEN TRACE THE NUMBERS AND WORDS.

1 ONE

PENCIL CASE

2 TWO

BACKPACKS

3 THREE

BOOKS

4 FOUR

PENCILS

5 FIVE

ERASERS

2 COUNT AND MATCH.

1

phive2015/iStockphoto.com

2

GlobalP/iStockphoto.com

3

Jamakosy/ iStockphoto.com

4

AlexLMX/iStockphoto.com

5

nico_blue/iStockphoto.com

3 LOOK AND CIRCLE.

A) 2 – TWO ELEPHANTS.

Lisa Lebedeva/iStockphoto.com

B) 4 – FOUR PIGS.

Carolina Sartório

C) 1 – ONE DOG.

golykim/iStockphoto.com

ENGLISH AROUND THE WORLD

CHILD'S PLAY

1 PLAYS FOR KIDS!

KIDS IN ENGLISH-SPEAKING COUNTRIES PLAY GAMES SIMILAR TO OURS. LOOK!

wundervisuals/iStockphoto.com

HOPSCOTCH.

SerrNovik/iStockphoto.com

HIDE-AND-SEEK.

shironosov/iStockphoto.com

BROKEN TELEPHONE.

FatCamera/iStockphoto.com

TAG.

VOCABULARY

HOPSCOTCH: AMARELINHA.
BROKEN TELEPHONE: TELEFONE SEM FIO.
HIDE-AND-SEEK: ESCONDE-ESCONDE.
TAG: PEGA-PEGA.

GOOD DEED

PLAYING WITH FRIENDS

- HOW NICE IT IS TO PLAY WITH FRIENDS WITH RESPECT AND CARE.

Nagaiets/iStockphoto.com

DIGITAL PLAY

CREATING A GAME

- CREATE A GAME WITH NUMBERS.

1. CREATE THE RULES.
2. PLAY WITH FRIENDS.
3. MAKE A MOVIE WITH YOUR CELL PHONE.

Kuzmina/Shutterstock.com

LET'S SING!

LEMON, LIME

LEMON, LIME,
BE ON TIME.
WHAT TIME DOES THE PARTY START?
ONE, TWO, THREE, FOUR, FIVE!

TRADITIONAL NURSERY RHYME.

Ideario Lab

VOCABULARY

LEMON: LIMÃO-SICILIANO.
LIME: LIMÃO.
BE ON TIME: SEJA PONTUAL.
WHAT TIME: QUE HORAS.
PARTY: FESTA.
START (TO START): COMEÇA (COMEÇAR).

LET'S

LISTEN

1 LISTEN AND COLOR.

Ideario Lab

LET'S PLAY

1 COUNT AND TRACE.

A) 

Ilustrações: Carolina Sartório

FOUR ORANGES

B) 

ONE ELEPHANT

C) 

TWO UMBRELLAS

D) 

THREE ICE CREAM CONES

E) 

TWO BOYS

2 COUNT, CIRCLE, AND COLOR.

1 – ONE	2 – TWO	3 – THREE	4 – FOUR	5 – FIVE

Bambrilla Ilustra

AFTER THIS UNIT

I CAN

COUNT THE NUMBERS FROM 1 TO 5 IN ENGLISH.

IDENTIFY NUMBERS AND QUANTITIES.

RESPECT MY FRIENDS DURING GAMES.

UNIT 4

MY SCHOOL

VOCABULARY

SCHOOL: ESCOLA.
LIKE (TO LIKE): GOSTO (GOSTAR).
VERY MUCH: MUITO.
TEACHER: PROFESSORA.
NICE: LEGAL, SIMPÁTICO(A), AMÁVEL.

LET'S PLAY

1 LOOK AND TRACE.

GOOD
MORNING

GOOD
AFTERNOON

GOOD
EVENING

GOOD
NIGHT

2 CIRCLE THE TEACHER AND COLOR THE PICTURE.

VOCABULARY

GOOD MORNING: BOM DIA.

LET'S LISTEN

1 LISTEN. THEN COLOR THE OBJECTS.

LET'S PLAY

1 TRACE THE WORDS.

DESK

SCHOOL

TEACHER

2 HELP JAY WITH HIS SCHOOL MATERIAL. MATCH.

Ideario Lab

BOOKS

AngelicaMari79/Shutterstock.com

PENCIL SHARPENER

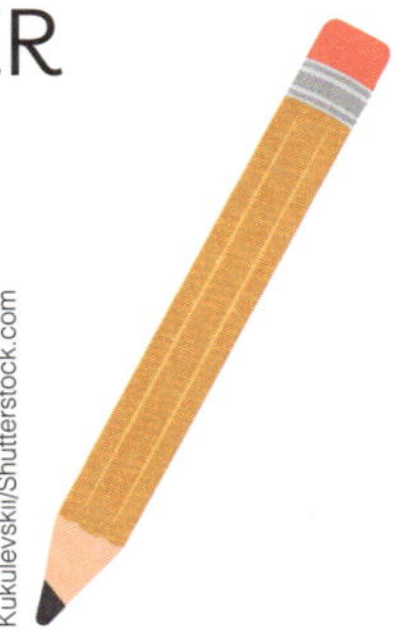
Kukulevskii/Shutterstock.com

PENCIL

Ideario Lab

Yaroslav Myronov/iStockphoto.com

ilterriorm/Shutterstock.com

CAR

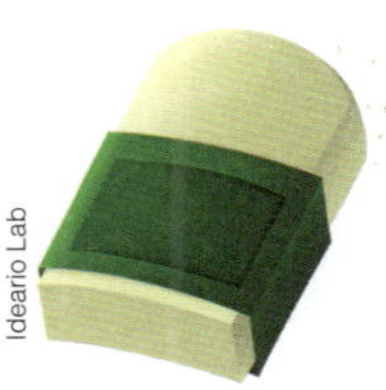
Ideario Lab

ERASER

BeataGFX/Shutterstock.com

APPLE

3 COUNT AND CHECK.

A)

Good Job/Shutterstock.com

- [ ] TWO
- [ ] THREE
- [ ] FOUR

B)

lightkitegirl/iStockphoto.com

- [ ] TWO
- [ ] THREE
- [ ] FOUR

C)

NikitaDesign/Shutterstock.com

- [ ] THREE
- [ ] FOUR
- [ ] FIVE

D)

Irisimka/iStockphoto.com

- [ ] ONE
- [ ] TWO
- [ ] THREE

ENGLISH
AROUND THE WORLD

GREETINGS AROUND THE WORLD: ENGLAND AND AUSTRALIA

- MATCH.

petch one/Shutterstock.com

ENGLISH FLAG.

Keanu/Shutterstock.com

AUSTRALIAN FLAG.

ARVO!

GOOD AFTERNOON!

DIGITAL PLAY

COUNTRY FLAGS

- CHOOSE THE FLAG OF YOUR COUNTRY.

petch one/Shutterstock.com

Keanu/Shutterstock.com

Leonidas Santana/Shutterstock.com

LET'S PLAY

1 LOOK AND FIND FIVE DIFFERENCES.

Ideario Lab

LET'S SING!

HOW MANY?

IT'S COUNTING TIME!
SO LET'S SING THIS RIGHT!

HOW MANY PENCILS IN A ROW?
LET'S COUNT THEM SLOWLY!
ONE, TWO, THREE, FOUR, FIVE!
FIVE LITTLE PENCILS IN A ROW!

HOW MANY ERASERS IN A ROW?
LET'S COUNT THEM SLOWLY!
ONE, TWO, THREE, FOUR, FIVE!
FIVE LITTLE ERASERS IN A ROW!

HOW MANY BOOKS IN A ROW?
LET'S COUNT THEM SLOWLY!
ONE, TWO, THREE, FOUR, FIVE!
FIVE LITTLE BOOKS IN A ROW!

SPECIALLY WRITTEN FOR THIS WORK.

DKO Estúdio

VOCABULARY

TIME: HORA.
RIGHT: CERTO.
ROW: FILA.
COUNT (TO COUNT): CONTAR.
SLOWLY: DEVAGAR.

GOOD DEED

BE A REAL FRIEND!

- HOW CAN WE BE A REAL FRIEND?

FamVeld/Shutterstock.com

AFTER THIS UNIT

I CAN

SAY GOOD MORNING, GOOD AFTERNOON, AND GOOD EVENING.			
NAME SCHOOL OBJECTS AND MATERIALS.			
GET TO KNOW THE FLAGS OF BRAZIL, AUSTRALIA, AND ENGLAND.			
VALUE ATTITUDES RELATED TO EMPATHY.			

UNIT 5

MY BODY

VOCABULARY

LOOK HERE: OLHE AQUI.

WHAT ARE YOU DOING?: O QUE VOCÊ ESTÁ FAZENDO?

MY BODY: MEU CORPO.

MY HANDS: MINHAS MÃOS.

MY FEET: MEUS PÉS.

LET'S PLAY

1 COLOR.

Ideario Lab

2 LOOK AND CHECK.

WHAT DID ERIC PAINT?

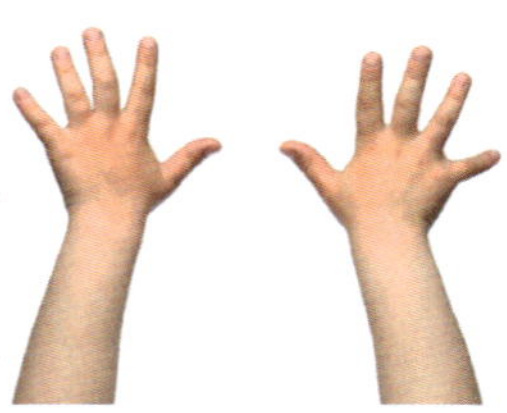
penyushkin/iStockphoto.com

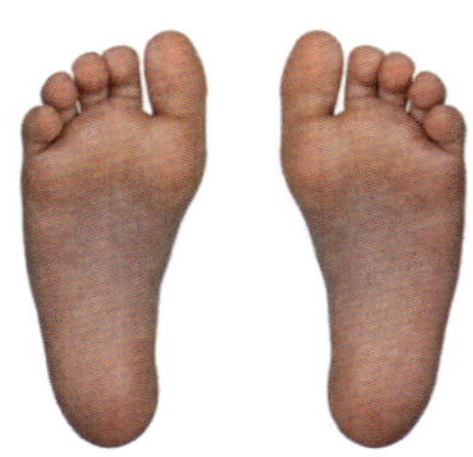
Dimedrol68/iStockphoto.com

AaronAmat/iStockphoto.com

☐ HIS HANDS. ☐ HIS FEET. ☐ A HEAD.

WHAT DID MIA PAINT?

AnaBoo/ Shutterstock.com

tuananh2121/Shutterstock.com

☐ A GIRL. ☐ A HOUSE AND A TREE.

3 MATCH.

HEAD

FACE

SHOULDER

LEG

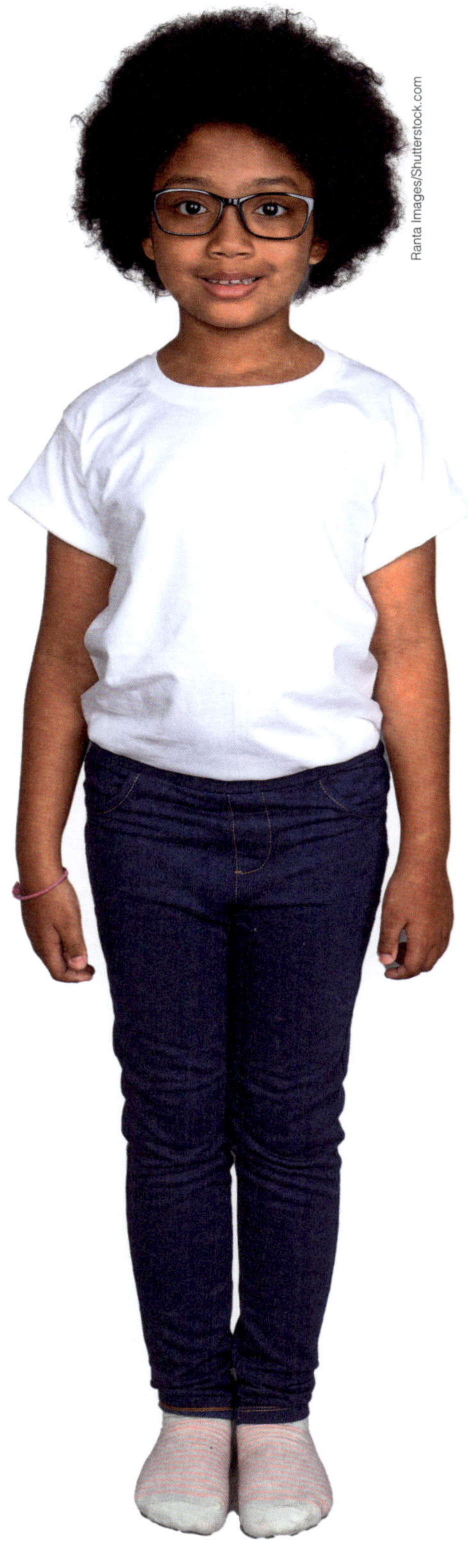

Ranta Images/Shutterstock.com

ARM

BELLY

HAND

FOOT

LET'S LISTEN

1 THESE ARE OUR BODY PARTS.

Ideario Lab

ARM

LEG

HEAD

HAND

Ideario Lab

SHOULDER

FOOT

FACE

LET'S PLAY

1 TRACE THE WORD.

maroke/iStockphoto.com

BODY

LET'S LISTEN

1 LISTEN AND COLOR.

HAND

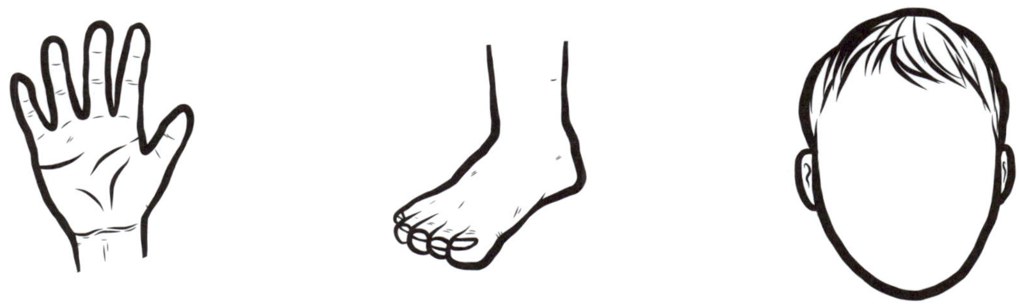

FOOT

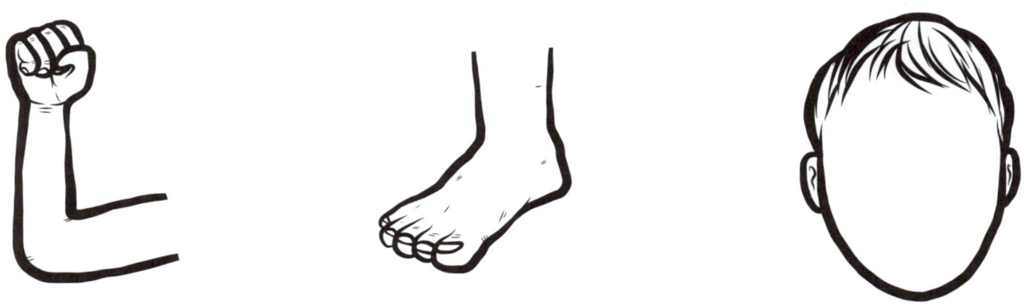

LEG

ARM

ENGLISH AROUND THE WORLD

GREETINGS AROUND THE WORLD

1 LOOK AND DRAW.

CIRCLE: JAPANESE CULTURE

TRIANGLE: THAI CULTURE

SQUARE: AMERICAN CULTURE

Ababsolutum/iStockphoto.com

Drazen Zigic/iStockphoto.com

MIA Studio/Shutterstock.com

LET'S SING!

HEAD AND SHOULDERS

HEAD, SHOULDERS, KNEES, AND TOES,
KNEES AND TOES
HEAD, SHOULDERS, KNEES, AND TOES,
KNEES AND TOES.

EYES AND EARS AND MOUTH AND NOSE.
HEAD, SHOULDERS, KNEES, AND TOES,
KNEES AND TOES.

NURSERY RHYME.

Ideario Lab

VOCABULARY

HEAD: CABEÇA.
SHOULDERS: OMBROS.
KNEES: JOELHOS.
TOES: DEDOS DOS PÉS.
EYES: OLHOS.
EARS: ORELHAS.
MOUTH: BOCA.
NOSE: NARIZ.

GOOD DEED

WASH YOUR HANDS!

1

WATER AND SOAP

2

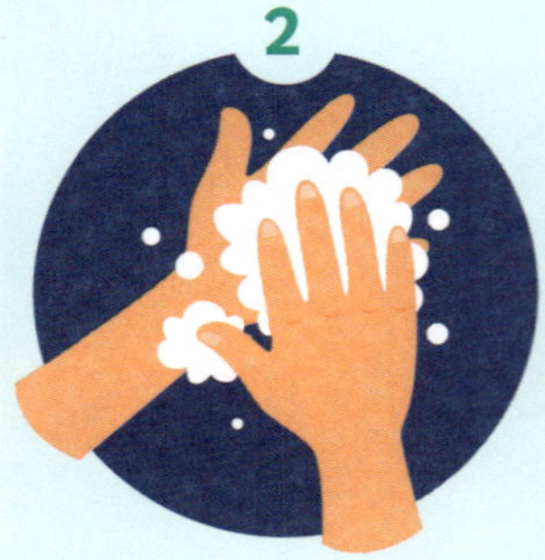

PALM TO PALM

3

BETWEEN FINGERS

yusufdemirci/Shutterstock.com

4

FOCUS ON THUMBS

5

BACK OF HANDS

6

FOCUS ON WRISTS

VOCABULARY

WATER: ÁGUA.

SOAP: SABÃO.

PALM TO PALM: PALMA A PALMA.

BETWEEN FINGERS: ENTRE OS DEDOS.

FOCUS ON THUMBS: ATENÇÃO AOS POLEGARES.

BACK OF HANDS: COSTAS DAS MÃOS.

FOCUS ON WRISTS: ATENÇÃO AOS PULSOS.

DIGITAL PLAY

LET'S PLAY A GAME!

- LISTEN TO YOUR TEACHER'S INSTRUCTIONS.

MIA Studio/Shutterstock.com

LET'S PLAY

1 CIRCLE THE BODY PARTS.

Ilustrações: Claudia Marianno

LET'S PLAY

1 PASTE THE STICKER.

AFTER THIS UNIT I CAN

IDENTIFY BODY PARTS.			
RECOGNIZE THE IMPORTANCE OF HYGIENE.			
LEARN GREETING GESTURES.			
IDENTIFY COLORS, QUANTITIES, AND NUMERALS.			

A HEALTHY SNACK

UNIT 6

VOCABULARY

GOOD AFTERNOON: BOA TARDE.
SNACK: LANCHE.
COOL: LEGAL.
LOVE (TO LOVE): AMO (AMAR).
FRUIT: FRUTA(S).
DELICIOUS: DELICIOSAS.
HEALTHY: SAUDÁVEIS.

LET'S LISTEN

1 LOOK AND LISTEN. THEN CIRCLE YOUR FAVORITE FRUIT.

Andrey Elkin/iStockphoto.com

WATERMELON

OSINSKIH AGENCY/iStockphoto.com

MANGO

Olexandra Yashechkina/iStockphoto.com

PEAR

Marat Musabirov/iStockphoto.com

BANANA

Olexandra Yashechkina/ iStockphoto.com

PAPAYA

Samohin/iStockphoto.com

APPLE

LET'S PLAY

1 MATCH THE FRUIT.

APPLE

PAPAYA

MANGO

PEAR

BANANA

WATERMELON

LET'S LISTEN

1 LISTEN, COUNT, AND MATCH.

bergamont/iStockphoto.com

APPLES

Roman Samokhin/iStockphoto.com

PEACH

kaanates/iStockphoto.com

PEARS

Josef Mohyla/iStockphoto.com

MELONS

Kuzma/iStockphoto.com

BANANAS

- ONE – 1
- TWO – 2
- THREE – 3
- FOUR – 4
- FIVE – 5

LET'S SING!

FIVE RED APPLES

FIVE RED APPLES IN A TREE
ONE LOOKED DOWN AT ME.
I SHOOK THE TREE
AND ONE FELL DOWN... IT WAS YUMMY!

FOUR RED APPLES IN A TREE,
ONE LOOKED DOWN AT ME.
I SHOOK THE TREE
AND ONE FELL DOWN... IT WAS YUMMY!

THREE RED APPLES IN A TREE,
ONE LOOKED DOWN AT ME.
I SHOOK THE TREE
AND ONE FELL DOWN... IT WAS YUMMY!
[...]

TRADITIONAL NURSERY RHYME.

Ideario Lab

VOCABULARY

TREE: ÁRVORE.

LOOKED DOWN (TO LOOK DOWN): OLHOU PARA BAIXO (OLHAR PARA BAIXO).

SHOOK (TO SHAKE): BALANCEI (BALANÇAR).

FELL DOWN (TO FALL DOWN): CAIU (CAIR).

LET'S PLAY

1. LOOK AND COLOR.

1 – RED   2 – ORANGE   3 – GREEN   4 – YELLOW

Ideario Lab

2 WATER AND FRUIT ARE HEALTHY! COLOR.

Ideario Lab

3 MARK THE PEARS.

Brambilla Ilustra

HOW MANY PEARS ARE THERE?

LET'S PLAY

1 HELP THE KIDS GET TO THEIR FAVORITE FRUIT.

DIGITAL PLAY

HEALTHY LIFE

- WHAT DO YOU EAT FOR MEALS?

Drazen Zigic/Shutterstock.com

AFTER THIS UNIT

I CAN

IDENTIFY SOME FRUIT.			
RECOGNIZE THE IMPORTANCE OF FRUIT AND WATER FOR A HEALTHY LIFE.			
UNDERSTAND THE IMPORTANCE OF A HEALTHY LIFE.			
IDENTIFY COLORS, QUANTITIES, AND NUMERALS.			
LEARN HOW TO USE *HOW MANY*.			

UNIT 7

MY FAMILY

Ideario Lab

VOCABULARY

HOUSE: CASA.
FAMILY: FAMÍLIA.
FATHER: PAI.
MOTHER: MÃE.
SISTER: IRMÃ.
BABY: BEBÊ.
BROTHER: IRMÃO.

LET'S PLAY

1 THIS IS AVA'S FAMILY. LOOK AND COLOR.

FATHER MOTHER SISTER BABY BROTHER

Ideario Lab

LET'S LISTEN

1 LISTEN AND CIRCLE. WHERE DOES AVA LIVE?

Roman Babakin/Shutterstock.com

IN A BUILDING.

Slavun/Shutterstock.com

IN A BIG HOUSE.

Joseph Hendrickson/Shutterstock.com

IN A SMALL HOUSE.

2 FIND OUT AND CIRCLE. WHERE DOES JAY LIVE?

IN AN APARTMENT BUILDING.

IN A HOUSE.

Ideario Lab

3 LISTEN AND FOLLOW THE INSTRUCTIONS.

THIS IS MIA'S FAMILY.

4 TRACE THE WORDS.

MOTHER

FATHER

BROTHER

SISTER

LET'S PLAY

1 DRAW YOUR FAMILY.

Claudia Marianno

GOOD DEED

RESPECT YOUR FAMILY!

1 LOOK AT THE PICTURE.

bbernard/Shutterstock.com

2 TRACE THE WORD.

FAMILY

LET'S PLAY

1 PASTE THE STICKERS IN THE RECYCLABLE GARBAGE.

lotos_land/Shutterstock.com

LET'S SING!

THIS IS MY FAMILY

THIS IS MY FAMILY.
LET'S COUNT THEM AND SEE
HOW MANY THERE ARE,
AND WHO THEY CAN BE.

THIS IS MY MOTHER,
WHO LOVES EVERYONE.
AND THIS IS MY FATHER,
WHO IS LOTS OF FUN.

THIS IS MY SISTER.
SHE HELPS AND SHE PLAYS.
AND THIS IS THE BABY,
HE SLEEPS ALL DAY.
AND THIS IS ME,
WHO SINGS AND WHO YOU SEE.

TRADITIONAL NURSERY RHYME.

Ideário Lab

VOCABULARY

COUNT (TO COUNT): CONTE (CONTAR).

SEE (TO SEE): VEJA (VER).

HOW MANY: QUANTOS.

WHO: QUEM.

EVERYONE: TODO MUNDO, TODOS.

HELPS (TO HELP): AJUDA (AJUDAR).

SLEEPS (TO SLEEP): DORME (DORMIR).

DIGITAL PLAY

MY FAMILY, MY HOME!

- WHO'S YOUR FAMILY?

Monkey Business Images/Shutterstock.com

ENGLISH AROUND THE WORLD

1 LOOK AND TRACE THE WORDS.

iampaese/Shutterstock.com

BIG HOUSE.

Artazum/Shutterstock.com

SMALL HOUSE.

Nayiya Kurmykova/Shutterstock.com

OLD HOUSE.

QinJin/Shutterstock.com

NEW BUILDING.

LET'S PLAY

1 FIND FOUR DIFFERENCES BETWEEN THE PICTURES.

2 CHECK THE **BIG** BUILDING.

mirjanajovic/iStockphoto.com

☐ ☐

AFTER THIS UNIT

I CAN

	😄	😐	😣
IDENTIFY MEMBERS IN A FAMILY.			
UNDERSTAND THE DIFFERENCES AND SIMILARITIES AMONG FAMILIES.			
USE THE ADJECTIVES *SMALL*, *BIG*, *NEW*, AND *OLD*.			
USE *THIS IS* AND *WHO*.			

UNIT 8

THE PAINTING

VOCABULARY

I LIKE: EU GOSTO.
I LOVE: EU AMO.
PAINTING: QUADRO.

LET'S PLAY

1 COLOR ACCORDING TO THE CODE.

1 - ORANGE 2 - YELLOW 3 - GREEN 4 - BLUE

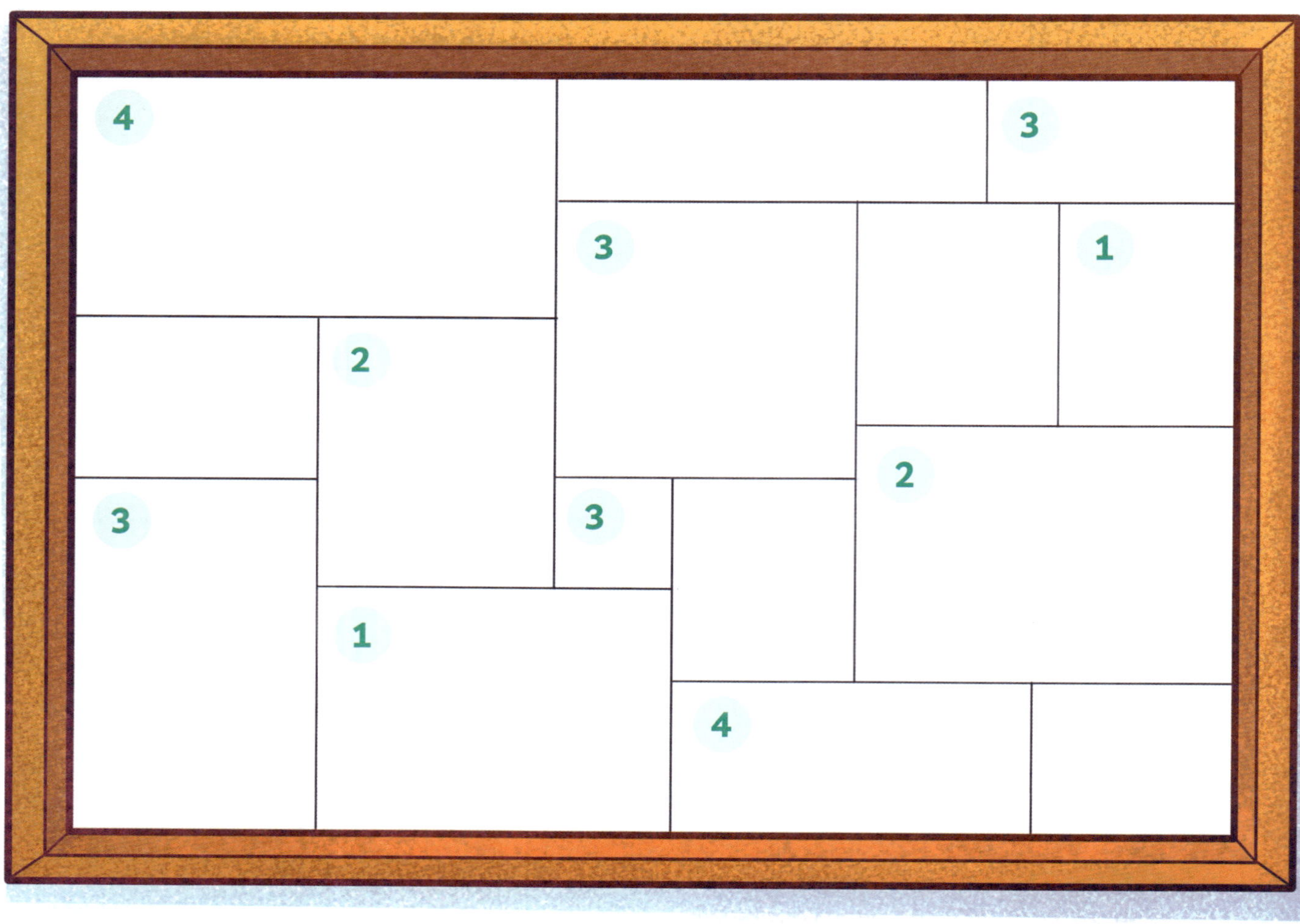

Ideario Lab

2 WHAT IS THE COLOR? CIRCLE.

TIM IS WEARING GREEN.

ERIC IS WEARING RED.

MIA IS WEARING BLUE.

AVA IS WEARING YELLOW.

3 TRACE THE WORDS.

Tartila/ Shutterstock.com

GREEN

RED

BLUE

YELLOW

LET'S LISTEN

1 LISTEN, REPEAT, AND MATCH.

A) THIS IS **BLACK**.
THIS IS A **DOG**.
THIS IS A **BLACK DOG**.

B) THIS IS **WHITE**.
THIS IS A **CAT**.
THIS IS A **WHITE CAT**.

C) THIS IS **YELLOW**.
THIS IS A **BIRD**.
THIS IS A **YELLOW BIRD**.

D) THIS IS **RED**.
THIS IS A **BUTTERFLY**.
THIS IS A **RED BUTTERFLY**.

tracielouise/iStockphoto.com

ProteanVisuals/iStockphoto.com

Seregraff/iStockphoto.com

MirasWonderland/Shutterstock.com

LET'S SING!

IF YOU ARE WEARING...

IF YOU ARE WEARING RED,
SHAKE YOUR HEAD.
IF YOU ARE WEARING RED,
THEN SHAKE YOUR HEAD.

VOCABULARY

WEARING (TO WEAR): VESTINDO (VESTIR).

SHAKE (TO SHAKE): BALANCE (BALANÇAR).

HEAD: CABEÇA.

IF YOU ARE WEARING BLUE,
TOUCH YOUR SHOE.
IF YOU ARE WEARING BLUE,
THEN TOUCH YOUR SHOE.

IF YOU ARE WEARING BLACK,
PAT YOUR BACK.
IF YOU ARE WEARING BLACK,
THEN PAT YOUR BACK.

IF YOU ARE WEARING BROWN,
TURN AROUND.
IF YOU ARE WEARING BROWN,
THEN TURN AROUND.

TRADITIONAL NURSERY RHYME.

Ideario Lab

VOCABULARY

TOUCH (TO TOUCH): TOQUE (TOCAR).
SHOE: SAPATO.
PAT (TO PAT): DÊ UM TAPINHA (DAR UM TAPINHA).
BACK: COSTAS.
TURN AROUND (TO TURN AROUND): VIRE (VIRAR).

GOOD DEED

COLORS THAT HELP PROTECT NATURE

- COLOR ACCORDING TO THE CAPTION.

BROWN — ORGANIC

YELLOW — METAL

BLUE — PAPER

H Art/Shutterstock.com

RED — PLASTIC

GREEN — GLASS

DIGITAL PLAY

VIRTUAL TOUR

- GO ON A VIRTUAL TOUR OF THE NATURAL HISTORY MUSEUM IN LONDON! THEN CONNECT THE DOTS.

abbydesign/Shutterstock.com

ENGLISH

AROUND THE WORLD

THE UNITED STATES FLAG

- LOOK AND COLOR THE FLAG OF THE UNITED STATES OF AMERICA.

nattiyapp/Shutterstock.com

nattiyapp/ Shutterstock.com

AFTER THIS UNIT

I CAN

IDENTIFY THE COLORS GREEN, BLUE, YELLOW, RED, BLACK, AND WHITE.

LEARN THE NAMES OF SOME ANIMALS IN ENGLISH.

USE *THIS IS*.

REVIEW

UNIT 1

1 TRACE THE WORDS **GIRL** AND **BOY**.

DenisNata/Shutterstock.com

GIRL

Harm Kruyshaar/Shutterstock.com

BOY

REVIEW

UNIT 2

1 TRACE AND COLOR.

APPLE

Saylee Rampurikar/Shutterstock.com

ELEPHANT

Kid_Games_Catalog/Shutterstock.com

ICE CREAM

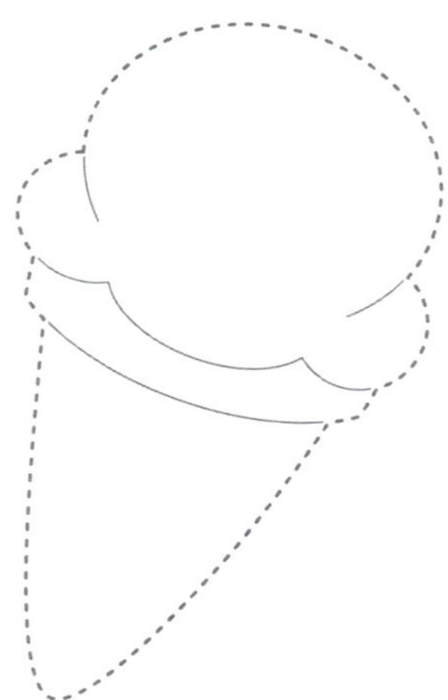

Kid_Games_Catalog/Shutterstock.com

ORANGE

Waqasnaseem2021/Shutterstock.com

UMBRELLA

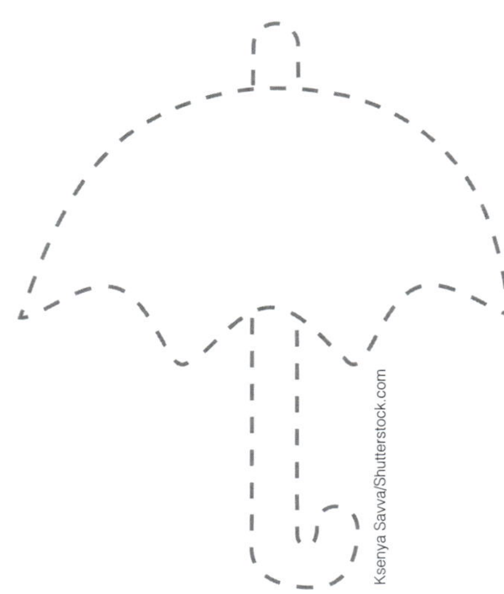

Ksenya Savva/Shutterstock.com

UNIT 3

1 MATCH FRUIT WITH NUMBERS.

jamakosy/Shutterstock.com

1 – ONE PAPAYA

Armas Vladimir/Shutterstock.com

5 – FIVE MANGOES

Dionisvera/Shutterstock.com

3 – THREE WATERMELONS

Binh Thanh Bui/Shutterstock.com

4 – FOUR PEACHES

Sergio33/Shutterstock.com

2 – TWO ORANGES

2 TRACE THE NUMBERS.

GoodFocused/Shutterstock.com

1 1 1 1 1 1

Thomas Leirikh/Shutterstock.com

2 2 2 2 2

irin-k/Shutterstock.com

3 3 3 3 3

grey_and/Shutterstock.com

4 4 4 4 4

phive/Shutterstock.com

5 5 5 5 5

UNIT 4

1 TRACE AND COLOR.

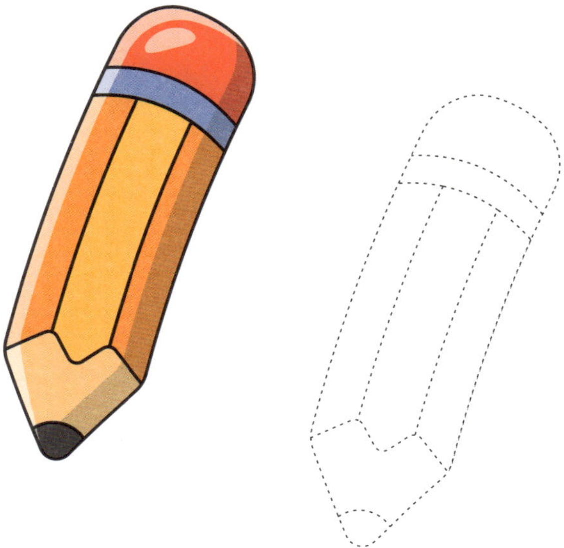

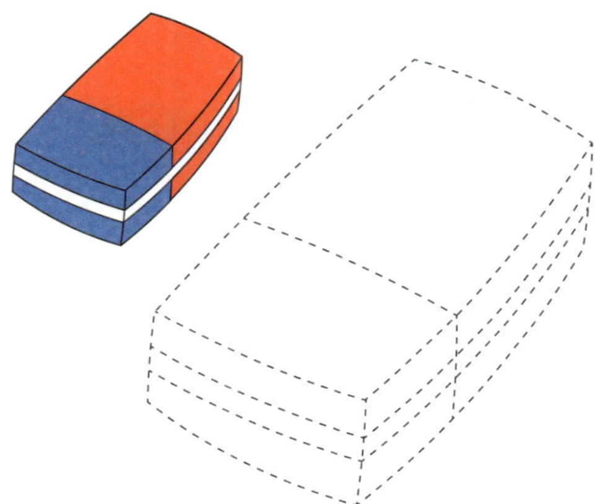

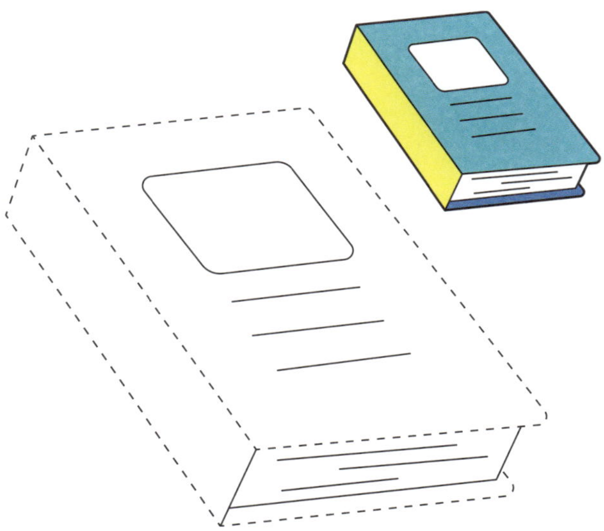

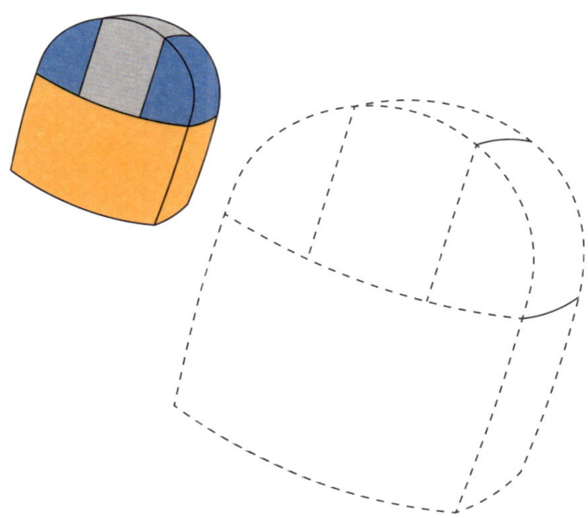

Ilustrações: fuatprasetya/Shutterstock.com

REVIEW

UNIT 5

1 LOOK AND MATCH THE PICTURES.

Ilustrações: Ideario Lab

MOTHER

LEGS

SISTER

SHOULDERS

BROTHER

FEET

FATHER

ARM

UNIT 6

1 TRACE THE WORDS.

magr80/Shutterstock.com

PEAR

Maks Narodenko/Shutterstock.com

BANANA

Good Job/Shutterstock.com

APPLE

Photoongraphy/ Shutterstock.com

ORANGE

UNIT 7

1 FIND THE WAY.

Ilustrações: Ideario Lab

2 TRACE THE WORDS.

Ground Picture/Shutterstock.com

FATHER

Cast Of Thousands/Shutterstock.com

MOTHER

PeopleImages.com - Yuri A/Shutterstock.com

SISTER

Lopolo/Shutterstock.com

BROTHER

REVIEW

UNIT 8

1 COLOR THE PICTURES.

PEAR

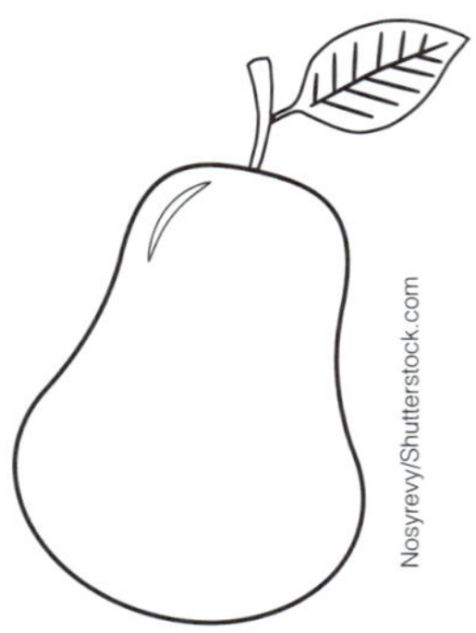

Nosyrevy/Shutterstock.com

APPLE

Nosyrevy/Shutterstock.com

WATERMELON

Kid_Games_Catalog/Shutterstock.com

PINEAPPLE

Kid_Games_Catalog/Shutterstock.com

PICTURE DICTIONARY

A

Carolina Sartório

AIRPLANE

Bruno Okada

ANT

Carolina Sartório

APPLE

Andrey1005/Shutterstock.com

ALLIGATOR

B

Ideario Lab

BABY

Bruno Okada

BALL

Janete Trindade

BANANA

Patricia Paulozi

BICYCLE

Bruno Okada

BIRD

Bruno Okada

BLACK

Patricia Paulozi

BLACKBOARD

Bruno Okada

BLUE

Ideario Lab

BODY

Luiz Lentini

BOOK

Bruno Okada

BOY

Bruno Okada

BREAKFAST

DKO Estúdio

BROTHER

Bruno Okada

BROWN

Ideario Lab

BUILDING

Bruno Okada

BUTTERFLY

C

Patricia Paulozi

CAR

Bruno Okada

CAT

Patricia Paulozi

CHAIR

Patricia Paulozi

CHALK

Carolina Sartório

CLASSROOM

D

Patricia Paulozi

DESK

Bruno Okada

DOG

Patricia Paulozi

DOLL

E

Carolina Sartório

EAGLE

Carolina Sartório

EGG

Carolina Sartório

ELEPHANT

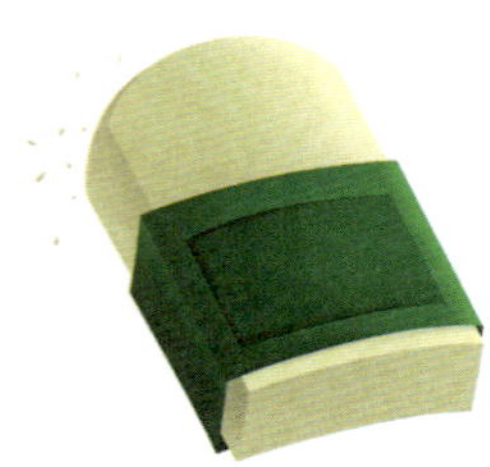

Carolina Sartório

ERASER

F

Ideario Lab

FAMILY

Maira Nakazaki

FATHER

DKO Estúdio

FISH

Bruno Okada

FIVE

Luiz Lentini

FLOWER

Bruno Okada

FOUR

Bruno Okada

FRUIT

G

Bruno Okada

GIRL

Bruno Okada

GREEN

H

Janete Trindade

HOUSE

I

Carolina Sartório

ICE CREAM

Carolina Sartório

IGLOO

Carolina Sartório

IGUANA

Carolina Sartório

INSECT

K

Maíra Nakazaki

KITCHEN

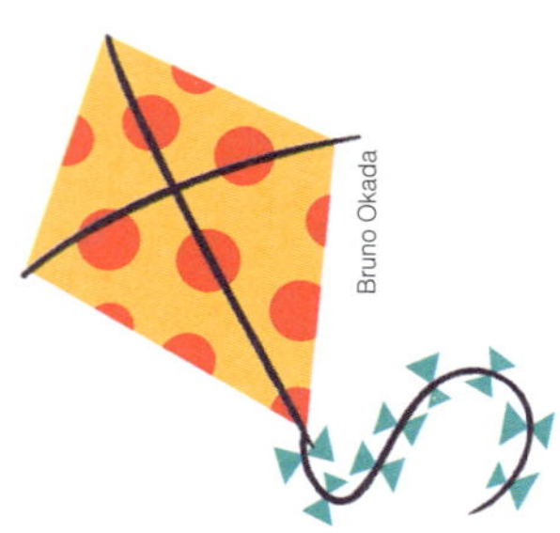

Bruno Okada

KITE

M

Janete Trindade

MANGO

Patricia Paulozi

MARBLES

Janete Trindade

MELON

Bruno Okada

MOTHER

O

Carolina Sartório

OCTOPUS

Carolina Sartório

ONION

Carolina Sartório

ORANGE

Carolina Sartório

OWL

P

Janete Trindade

PAPAYA

Janete Trindade

PEACH

Janete Trindade

PEAR

Patricia Paulozi

PENCIL

R

Bruno Okada

RED

Bruno Okada

ROPE

S

Patricia Paulozi

SEESAW

Luiz Lentini

SHOE

DKO Estúdio

SISTER

Bruno Okada

SON

Marcelo Azalim

SUN

T

Bruno Okada

THREE

Patricia Paulozi

TOP

Bruno Okada

TWO

U

Carolina Sartório

UMBRELLA

V

Carolina Sartório

VEGETABLE

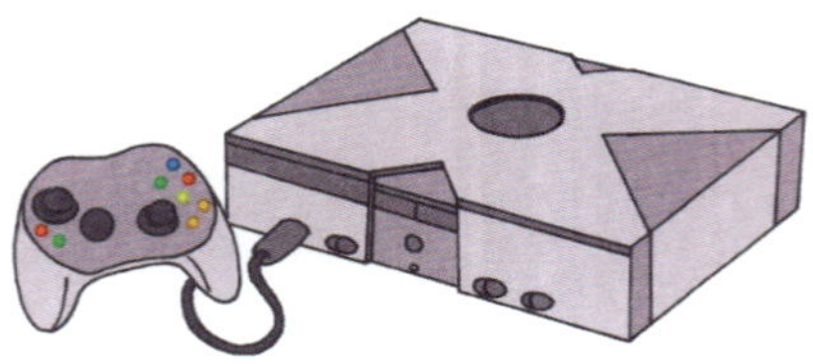

Patricia Paulozi

VIDEO GAME

W

Carolina Sartório

WATER

Janete Trindade

WATERMELON

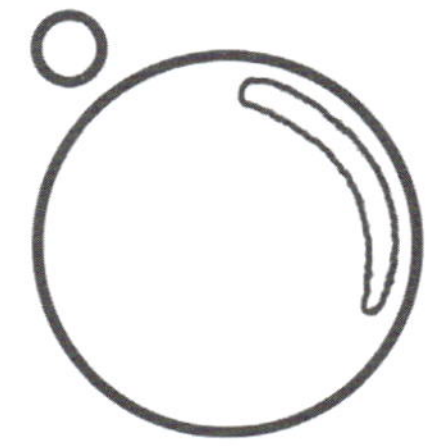

Bruno Okada

WHITE

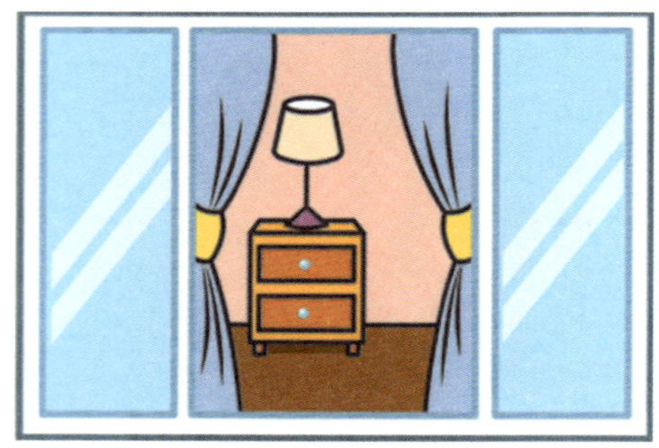

Janete Trindade

WINDOW

Y

Bruno Okada

YELLOW

INDEX OF SONGS

INDEX OF LISTENINGS

AUSTRALIA'S DAY

Flag'Stock/Shutterstock.com

VALENTINE'S DAY

INTERNATIONAL DAY OF FAMILIES

Claudia Marianno

EASTER

Claudia Marianno

MOTHER'S DAY

Claudia Marianno

FATHER'S DAY

Claudia Marianno

THANKSGIVING

Claudia Marianno

CHRISTMAS

Claudia Marianno

STICKERS

PAGE 8

Ilustrações: Ideario Lab

PAGE 21

Ilustrações: Claudia Marianno

PAGE 24

Ilustrações: Ideario Lab

PAGE 42

David Franklin/Shutterstock.com

CoolPhotoGirl/Shutterstock.com

ZaZa Studio/Shutterstock.com

Ahmet Misirligul/Shutterstock.com

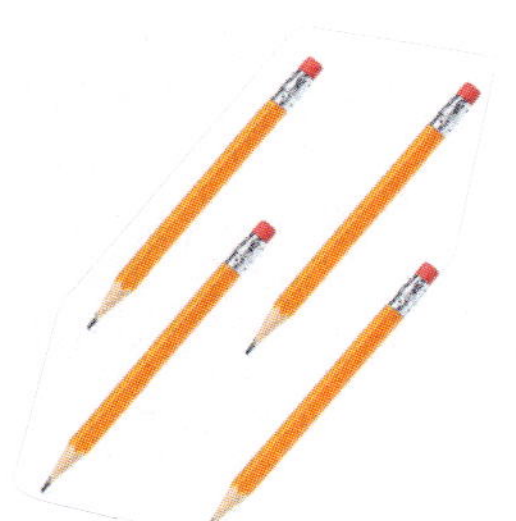

Birgit Reitz-Hofmann/Shutterstock.com

STICKERS

PAGE 74

Ideario Lab

PAGE 92

lotos_land/Shutterstock.com